Hidden Bloom

Sasha Sheppard

Entegrity Choice Publishing
PO Box 453
Powder Springs, GA 30127

Author photo by J. Phillips Media, LLC

Library of Congress Cataloging-in-Publication Data
ISBN 978-1-7351739-9-3
Library of Congress Control Number: 2020910951

Honorary Flower

I dedicate this book to my friend, Darius Jackson, who passed away at a young age to cancer in 2017. Darius, I promised you I would finish my story and let you read it when it was finished. Unfortunately, you passed away before you could even see the progress.

Darius was a leader, a fighter, an innovator, and he was also bound to be a world changer. He encouraged me many years ago to start telling my story and I told him to start on his. He made an impact on my life in more ways than one. Gone... but never forgotten!

Contents

Part I – Introduction

Part II – Seed

Part 1
Introduction

Introduction

I never thought I would be in this place of finding more of my hidden bloom and continuously finding it daily in spite of all the obstacles and disappointments that life sometimes brings. Not that I have it all together while beginning to write this book. I would be lying if I told you I did — and I still don't.

Life is what you make it and each day of your life brings new challenges, maybe new obstacles, and even the greatest things that may change you in one single day, one single moment, and even one single experience. It is those moments that we are presented with that develop us, strengthen us, and embody the depth of our very being.

This book is not meant to make you dwell on things that remind you of your past or cause you to become stagnated in where you are. It is an opportunity to look beyond whatever has happened in your life and bring clarity into the true purpose of your existence and your importance to the world.

Even in the midst of an uncertainty about where you are, I hope this book serves as a springboard toward healing, breakthrough, and development in order to become all that God has planned for you. I also hope that the real-life events that have happened to you permit you to embrace all that you have experienced and to share it with others.

Sharing your life with others can be quite intimidating because of the thoughts that run through your mind as to how your life story can be received in such a way that you won't be judged, ridiculed, and even dismissed. We hold back our stories because of the fear of being out there; exposed and vulnerable. If the truth be told, sharing our stories allows us to reflect on how far life has come about for us. Failure to release our stories robs the person who is waiting for our story so that they can ignite passion, change, and discovery in their own lives.

So, here I am — transparent and unrestrained — showing you a part of the transformation of my heart where the healing has begun.

Here is Hidden Bloom.

1
Discovering Your Hidden Bloom

Discovering one's hidden bloom starts simply with a seed that was planted and hidden until the time came for the flower to bloom. We can remain hidden because of what we don't want to see of ourselves. Our identity encompasses the good, the bad, the ugly, and sometimes even the gruesome — to the point where there is a thought of, "Oh, this isn't me." But it is. The question is what do you discover when life gives you the honest truth of your reality that cannot be hidden?

2
In Hiding

To be hidden is often described as to cover up, to be in disguise. But, often, it can be a place of seclusion for growth and protection from things or people that may be a hindrance. Without those hidden moments, you miss out on the opportunity to see who you really are and to be able to start the change you want to see — not only within you but in those who are around you.

3
To Bloom

To bloom is described as to be open, noticed, and confident. It is destined, however, for many attacks although they will not hinder you because they will stretch you. To embrace all that you are and all that you have been through should be displayed as something that has been worth keeping.

We all want something to keep that which has been tested, tried, and proven because it gives off a sense of strength, substance, and value. Knowing you are worth every bit of the truth of your story and your life will forever be the case because of one single seed that was the creation of you!

Part II
Seed

4
The Seed

Transformation of the seed does not truly begin until there is a possibility of something being ignited. It starts from the ground up. It never comes from the outside of something that is being created and it doesn't go back into the ground to expand and never come out to impact others. There is life beyond the ground, life beyond where you are, and life beyond the wait.

5

Hi, My Name Is . . .

**Before I formed you in your mother's womb
I chose you.**
Jeremiah 1:5 NET

From the very beginning of your existence, a blueprint was made for your destiny to be fulfilled. It's *much* harder than it sounds. You master your own destiny through life experiences and you develop into the person that you were created to be.

When you forget the reasons why you are on this earth, you tend to put yourself into areas that will not be conducive to the development of your purpose and assignment. This can often lead to discouragement, disappointment, and even some delays.

6
What Is A Seed?

A seed is composed of three different dimensions; the surface, the core, and the potential outcome. Nothing that is put into the ground at the very beginning of development loses any of its components nor does it lack its existence once it is put there.

Seeds have different shapes but the outcome of particular seeds depends upon the ways in which they develop and how much they can be exposed or hidden for their own preservation.

The seed is the beginning of creation for a specific purpose and a specific time that will impact the environment in which you live in. When you have a purpose, your life revolves around sustaining that purpose.

We are seeds that God has planted in the earth. There are no seeds that are exactly the same even though they may come from the same group: family, genetics, long generational curses of poverty, addiction, or abuse. Who we are or will become is a result of the seed that was planted in us.

7
Beyond the Surface

To understand something, you have to know the difference between what it appears to be and what it really is. A lot of times in our lives there are things that become more noticeable because we create images of what we believe others will see, or what we want others to see, and they might be hidden disguises but broken views.

How many times have you allowed how you were planted, when you were planted, and where you were planted to obstruct your view?

Behind our masks, we can't see all the broken pieces that surround us. In all honesty, it makes you want to keep things covered up. Masking is safe and eliminates the risk of being exposed to questions you do not want to answer.

There is the surface of a facade, or a masked image created from the start until life happens, that forces you to get cut, bruised, and even broken sometimes in order to go beyond the surface.

8

You Don't Get to Pick Where You Are Planted

As a native of New Orleans, Louisiana, I spent most of my childhood in a family that was protective, loving, and free spirited but I never imagined as a child what it would take for me to be here now.

Everyone in my family has experienced incredible hardships including physical abuse, poverty, neglect, substance abuse, mental illness, alcohol addiction, loss of those close to them because of murder, and many other things. I would love to share those experiences with you but that is only for them to share. Through it all, wisdom has been drawn from those experiences and has provided me with strength and a backbone.

The vertebrae are a very significant metaphor for the structure of a family. The vertebrae align to the structure of every part of the backbone and that represents a generation of those who overcome their experiences and become stronger with whatever life throws their way. Most of our weight is carried at the lower part of the spine and that is why the lower vertebrae are larger and more stable than the top vertebrae.

You have to carry your own weight regardless of the dynamics of the family structure in which you were born into. You do not get the pleasure of selecting your family.

The bigger the purpose, the bigger the tests.

The beginnings of my existence included much yearning for attention and validation. I often found myself being rebellious and outspoken to achieve those ends. I got lost in who I was because of the rejection I felt from others as a child. Oftentimes, I found myself hidden in my room in isolation but with an active imagination. In those times, I created a world of fantasy in my mind that did not coincide with my reality but it worked for me in those moments.

I remember the first time I felt rejection. I was in elementary school in the second grade. I had a huge first crush on a boy and believed that he was into me. He was in the third grade and the classes were normally combined in the school that I attended. I had this crush but I also had a best friend who knew of my crush. One day I got the courage to go up to the boy and say hello but it didn't work out too well. I kept wondering why he was so into my friend rather than me.

The next day my friend told me that he came over to her house because his parents had dropped him off. I was thinking that was the ultimate betrayal. I mean, at the time it wasn't funny and I stopped being friends with her because of it. As crazy as it may sound, there wasn't truly a rejection from others. There was the expectation of acceptance in my mind and it excluded the understanding of another's feelings about me.

That was the very first seed I planted. I didn't realize that my first planted seed would be recognized by many and that I would eventually go through life yearning for water, covering, and nourishment from others.

"You are beautiful" were the words my father said often. Never once did I doubt my reflection in the eyes of my dad because I never felt unwanted. He reminded me every day of how beautiful I am and that's all I knew.

It is impactful in a young girl's mind to have a father reinforce positive affirmations. However, the encounter with my second grade crush led me to believe that maybe the words my father often said weren't necessarily completely true because, after all, I only knew about my beauty.

That was the core of the beginning stages of my life. The core is defined as the portion of a foundry mold that shapes the interior of a hollow casting. I am not particularly defining the core of an existence as metal but the definition plays a significant role about shaping an empty space. I don't think I ever knew how to fill that empty space but I definitely was protected and my father made sure of that. However, he could not protect me from life as it happened.

Although my father tried, it didn't quite work out the way that he thought it would. In my youth, I was safe in my bubble but I did not understand the true impact of living inside of an overprotective bubble. It was much more than just not having a boyfriend until I was thirty or that I couldn't wear colored nail polish until I was sixteen. I was banned from wearing red lipstick; dad thought it made me look like a clown.

It was life that I wasn't prepared to live without my dad assuring me every step of the way and validating my every move. The validation that I continuously needed from him started from a desire to always do what was best for him in his eyes and yearning for attention when it was given elsewhere. I didn't realize that the validation I needed from him was all that he could give me. It wasn't his fault.

He married my mom at eighteen years old and started building a life for his family. Coming from a background of strong men who worked hard, took care of their women, and protected their family, was all that he knew. I honestly didn't really know at the time what I truly wanted from him. I only wanted to be in his sight. Not one material thing ever mattered for me. Not one particular outing mattered to me or the many times that he would be popping up at school unannounced and peeping through the classroom door to make sure I was on task. It was important just knowing that he saw me.

I remember when my dad used to work late mopping floors at the LSU buildings and sometimes, he would bring my sister and me along. He was always doing something but I knew that for me, sight was more important than the physical touch. When you see that you can embrace, you can appreciate that and you can see beyond the makeup. When you become blind to sight, you have to imagine and create a reality. In my mind, if I knew that you saw me, I would see myself.

As confusing as it may sound, I can honestly say I never saw myself. I was blindsided on the ideal relationship that I thought I didn't have but came to realize that I had it all along. It even challenged me in my life and my relationship with God because I couldn't really connect a father with God as a father because of the disconnect that I thought I had with my very own. I didn't realize he himself had a disconnect with his own.

Every day I woke up to develop my voice so that it would be strengthened to become louder and louder and heard instead of my feeling afraid to speak because of a quick rebuttal or shutdown. Yes, I was that curious child and I feel I will get payback in the future from my kids who will always ask, "Why?" I never felt I did anything right or was good enough in my dad's eyes. We are just alike in every way and at times it was good and at other times it wasn't the best. Our relationship wasn't something that could be explained. It was just experienced because everything he said was "clearly" right.

The view shifted and became clearer into that transition and continuation of yearning for validation from him. Something else that was quite simple yet had a meaningful impact on my life was my sister. She was my younger sister who was responsible, smart, and could eat her vegetables. Even now, she is the golden child. She ate all her vegetables and mine. I was not getting the nutrients that I needed to be strong like Popeye, the cartoon character that I would watch. I recall a time when we could not drink Kool-Aid or have desert if everything on our plate was not eaten. I used to sit in panic because I hated vegetables. I wished we had a dog so that I could feed my vegetables to the dog.

In my mind, I never wanted to be a bulky person with huge muscles so I thought that the nutrients didn't apply to me. I was the child who, if something wasn't a part of the makeup of who I thought I would become, I wouldn't let that change me. Even as a child, I knew I was different and that vegetables were my imprisonment. I would die from thirst before vegetables would shackle me from my true freedom of endless candy and eating what I wanted.

Oh yes, theatre became my stage. But that's beside the point. I remember sitting at the dinner table and my sister finishes her meal. I'm the only one left at the table in the dimly lit dining room and my parents are across the table and waiting for me to finish every bite. My plan was to fall asleep at the table and then I wouldn't have to eat my vegetables, and it worked. However, to my surprise, the next morning I was confronted with the same meal reheated for me to eat.

That was just too much for my young mind to experience. I couldn't even realize that the reason I would get frustrated at times was because things like that happened periodically. It was like I didn't want to face the things that would make me strong and that they would still show up the next day.

That's how life is sometimes. We get planted and then we sometimes don't like what we are being protected from. Or we don't like what we are given in order to grow. Oftentimes, we can delay our growth process that hinders our potential outcome.

The experiences with my father taught me more

things than I could have ever imagined. Like the time I preferred my dad to comb my hair rather than my mom because he had a more delicate touch. Dad could do a mean roller set. That's only because he had two younger sisters who he had to do hair for when they were younger. No shade to my mother. I just knew that with her hands I would definitely have that "surprised" look every time.

There was one time I was so sad as a child and my dad made me jump up and down yelling continuously, "I'm happy," until I started smiling. I don't think I ever told him about all of the moments I did appreciate with him. I think he knew that he didn't know everything but sometimes what I thought wasn't the best really was. The times in which my father did his best was the best he ever did. A father sees good things inside of you that you may not see in yourself. A good relationship also does not feed your desires of wanting things right away and leaves a path that is easy for you to access.

One thing about seeds, they are never tied down to anything, but scattered in places, where they are needed for purposeful growth. Anything without purpose can't grow.

9
I Planted The Seed

Throughout my life, I have looked to others for my success and failures with the definition of self-worth, identity, value, and even of substance. Imagine your life being defined in the hands of people who don't even know that you are literally giving them everything for the molding of your development.

Most are not even aware of your emptiness. We find ourselves planting seeds that others have created for what they project us to be when we don't even know ourselves what we want to be. We fail to realize that everything that is planted was never intended to be put in the dirt of our path. We need to allow ourselves to go against what frustrates our purpose and our assignments. Allowing broken people, lying people, depressing people, and the "takers" to have space in our environment causes us to lose the compass that navigates to a road to who we truly are.

Are there people, places, or things that you have held onto that are attached to fear, anger, or even unworthiness? Identify those things you have allowed to stay planted seeds so that they can fill in the voids. Be careful of what and who you attach yourself to, who you listen to, and even the things we often tell ourselves. If you are not careful with what you allow into your space, life will move whatever is planted. Just don't let it get to the root.

Part III
Thorns

10
Thorns

Many people experience heartbreak or disappointments and choose to go through life carrying the pain. Pain hurts but it is part of the growing process of life. Life is bittersweet. Thorns are not enjoyable but they are often necessary.

Imagine a cactus. The plant is surrounded by tiny pricks scattered all over the odd-shaped plant nonetheless, there is something unique inside the cactus. There is a refreshing amount of water springing from the inside of it in spite of the desert around it.

The desert in the day is humid and many times scorching hot but, as night falls, the cool breeze overshadows the day. That's an example of life. Life can appear at times to be dry, humid, and even unbearable but what sustains you is the thirst for more. A lot of people do not understand the purpose of a thorn.

Thorns are used for protection.

Thorns can operate from those deep and heart-tugging experiences in life that made you change the trajectory of how you see the world and how you see yourself. Thorns are displayed on the surface for the purpose of protecting the core of your being. Sometimes, even in the darkness, there is always a hidden light pushing you forward. It is operated from the experiences in life that are displayed on the surface to the core of your being. There may be some things that have happened to you that broke you into pieces to the point where you questioned the meaning of life and your purpose in it.

Hurt can carry burdens that are equipped with past reminders and emotional memory storage of replays. If you hold onto to them for a long period of time, it will start to affect you physically, mentally, spiritually, and emotionally. Hurt that is not managed can catch you off guard. Emotions can be bottled and yet scattered into many areas that you cannot handle or function in. That's where the battle takes place. The consumption of our hurts overrides the process in which we develop. We need to push through and give in to the lessons of life that are able to create thorns so that we can achieve strength and perseverance.

Holding onto thorns can only continue to remind you of your past and what you did or what others have done to you. If you allow the pricks to intimidate you, you will find yourself lost in the purpose beyond the thorn. This will make you believe that you are thirsty and have no access to the living water that is booming inside of you.

You need to not think so much about the drought of your pain but, instead, about the refreshing of your heartbeat that pumps every last drop of tears or balled fists that you may have created. There is no healing until there is a definite release or a sign of yielding to what you desire in order for restoration to take place.

11

Thorns In Isolation

"Hello. Is it okay if I can stay with you?"
"No." Closed door.

"I just need two weeks to stay."

"No." Closed door.

"How about you check into shelter options?"
Closed door. That is the last thing I remember my
mom saying. She even sent me an email with shelter listings and offered to drive me to them.

Have you ever been in a place where you felt you
were at rock bottom to the rock bottom? There may
be a different situation for you but I won't ever forget a time in my life when I had no place to go. I
didn't know what survival was until I had to learn
about it on my own.

There were many closed doors that I have faced
in life. I know what it feels like to be in a place of
hopelessness and defeat and looking for a way out.

I was devastated. I didn't know how I had gotten to that place. Well, I definitely do now.

At one point in my life, I was at a place where I didn't know where to go or who to turn to, including my own family. I was unprepared for the unexpected and that left me in a place of uncertainty and doubt. It's not like I was the child who was on drugs or out partying. Besides, I never skipped school even once. But it was just the stage of my growth that my parents didn't understand and I didn't either. It was like I was thrown into a world I knew nothing about because I always had a shield around me which later in life made me do adulting wrong.

I remember my dad once telling me, "You're better out of the house to figure it out because you trust God more there and it seems it works better for you when you're struggling." I kid you not, I honestly hated my parents at that point and I still at times feel resentment towards them. It's like sometimes our family feels like they know what is best for us, and sometimes it is for the best, but the way they communicate makes what they say worse than how they actually feel.

Although I was hurt, I had to understand that no one owes me anything. So, I had to struggle a lot of times to understand the strength that I truly had and I had to learn to grow up. My daily prayer that I honestly have with myself when it comes to my family is, "Lord, let me never resent them and let my heart not be hardened by what I hear or see." I repeat this prayer not just for my family but for my friends and anyone that I come in contact with.

12
Can I Survive?
I need a drink.

During one point in my ministry calling, I was on the tip of depression. I had lost touch with my true identity and went off balance to the point where I started to question scriptures and everything I had learned during my spiritual development. I became detached and disconnected to anything that would bring light into my life. I became so numb that the pain I felt superseded my mind. I was lost. I had no sense of destiny and didn't think it still belonged to me. I thought that a person with a Minister's collar couldn't receive grace because, "I should have known better."

I had given my flesh more than what my spirit could handle and at times that caused me to believe in anyone's voice and even more so a prayer. I had become frustrated that the tears flowed consistently. I mean hard with snot gushing from my nose. That's how much I didn't want to go through with it. I was so used to having someone always there who would pacify my downfalls as well as create a safe haven for my brokenness, worry, and even misjudgments.

My bitterness towards God and towards those around me was very apparent and evident. Honestly, I felt like I was a child all over again. When I couldn't get my way, I would become very dramatic even if that included going as far as sitting on the floor with my head down to seek attention. I promise you; it worked every time. Now it didn't but I had to go through the process.

Your process may not include tears that reminded you of your childhood but there may be something else that might arise over time. I worked countless hours and even picked up a second job at night to eliminate the darkness of failure that was constantly playing in my mind. Worry and brokenness at times led me into deep dark places. My face was hidden, my voice began to shake, and anxiety dominated my mind when I was asked how I was doing. I had an image to protect and I didn't want others to see that I did not have it all together. It was such an disguise that I convinced myself of my made-up identity.

Frequently, I applied eyeshadow so that no one could see or take notice of my eyes. I applied mascara only to bring a more dramatic appeal but no one knew what I was facing beyond the mascara because on many Sunday's I shouted and sang, "How great is our God" but in my heart, I felt empty and frustrated. There was a hidden voice inside of me saying, "How can God allow me to go through this?" I had a pity party with myself. Yes, with me.

When I was out of living options, I went to an extended stay hotel. I recall opening the door to my hotel room and seeing a bed, chair, TV, and a mini fridge with a stove top. When I entered the bathroom, I saw hair seeping through the drain and evidence on the shower glass of stray hair left behind. It wasn't the best situation but it was the best for that time. I grabbed some bleach, disinfectant, and every cleaning product I could think of so the room could be livable. I was thinking to myself, "I've got to make it out alive if I'm going to live through it."

As I sat in the dimly lit room with curtains closed because people were walking back and forth outside of my window, tears began to flow. My living option was sucking me dry emotionally, spiritually, and financially. I asked God, "Why is this happening to me? How can I see beyond where I am in this place?"

I had never been at a place where I was out of options and resources for help. That experience transformed my way of living. I was at rock bottom with no vision and no comfort. I was alone and talking my way through to my next blessing.

While I was going through this test, I kept reminding myself that I could live, grow and get through it with God's help. I was determined that this test was not going to be the end of me. At times, it took every ounce of hope that I could muster up to push me forward. Honestly, there were times in which I thought there was no way I could live through it. It was a road that I had to travel alone; no one could understand all that I was dealing with. In the end, God brought me through it.

There were many praise songs that got me through some tough times. Those songs reminded me that no matter what I face in life, I can get through it. When your faith is tested, endurance has a chance to grow. I believe wholeheartedly that life can throw you some curve balls that make you question everything. Even when you have moments when you thought they were the worst, because you pressed through it, you can testify to others how you made it.

Anytime you are in a place where you feel like you can't go another day experiencing the pain, remember that the pain will make you stronger in the end. Tests are hard at times but tests build stamina, character, integrity, and birth purpose. Testing teaches us what to do or what not to do. In my extended stay hotel experience, I knew it was simply a stepping stone to my next set destination.

God is full of surprises. Little did I know that a phone call about an apartment would change my circumstances. When I went to sign the lease, I discovered that it was a two bedroom, one and a half bath, townhouse – bigger than any place I had ever lived. God is definitely there for us in times of need.

Wherever your "extended stay" may be at the moment, remember that God is preparing you for a breakthrough.

13
Self-Inflicted Wounds

Not only are thorns used for protection, they are also used for warnings. I've experienced many things in my life that have led me to places because of disobedience or being at the wrong place at the wrong time. This chapter is probably one of the hardest to write. Honestly, at this very moment I am realizing the seriousness of things that I have swept under the rug in exchange for another's feelings.

A lot of times we place ourselves in the hands of others because of the image that we have created that contradicts what has happened to us. But in all honesty, it discombobulates our effectiveness and the need to truly feel free and whole within ourselves. I have definitely experienced a lot of heartache and heartbreak when it comes to relationships. Even friendships that I thought were for me turned out to be that only I was for me.

I went through many years of holding onto things with regret that I had no control over. In reality, I was trying to find any way that I could to get in control. I remember a painful experience like the back of my hand.

I got a phone call from a friend who I hadn't seen in a while. It was strange because I hadn't even communicated with that person in a good year or so. The last time I was in contact with that friend was at a party and he pushed me against a wall and the night ended with his people pulling a gun out on my family who were trying to defend me at the time.

I decided to go out with that person, not knowing what the day would entail, but I needed a break from life at that moment. Before I went out with him, I remember being in the bathroom putting makeup on. As I started to apply my eyeshadow, I heard clearly in my spirit, "Do not go out." I literally knew the voice and talked back to it like it was a friend standing next to me. I went back and forth and I kept hearing the same words, "Do not go out." I responded to the voice and said, "No, I deserve a break. I'm not going to be in my apartment cooped up and depressed with nowhere to go." Before leaving the house, I heard the same voice say again, "Do not go out."

I ditched the warning and went out for the night and that ended up being the biggest regret of my life. As I approached his car, everything about it was so off, even to the point where a drink was given to me uncovered. I took a sip of the drink not knowing what it was. As he was giving the drink to me, he said, "It's like communion." I did not understand the gravity of what was happening because I trusted this person. I had two more shots after that drink. I didn't want to drink much because I wanted to keep sane since I hadn't been around that guy for a while.

As the night ended, I got in the car and we headed back to my place. Quickly, my mind began to spin. I was sitting there like I didn't even drink anything. We arrived at my apartment but I sat in the car for a minute to get myself together to walk up the stairs. He insisted on walking me to my door to make sure I was safe and I told him that I was okay. I wasn't really thinking anything of it because I'd known that guy for years and there was nothing to caution me. One time in the past, I had too much to drink and he made sure I was good and he never once tried me. Despite that, the day was different.

I went up the stairs and into my apartment. I remember going into the bathroom, throwing up, and he was there. As I went back into the living room to lie down for a moment, I remember closing my eyes and opening them to a dark shadow. There was a foggy look to what was above me. I tried to fight it off but I didn't know what was going on. He was on top of me and seconds later I blacked out. I don't remember anything that happened after that moment.

I know that it was angels that were around me trying to get me up from the floor. As I opened my eyes, I saw a bright light and it was so bright that I had to put my hand across my face for a moment. In my drowsy state, I opened my eyes and said, "Why is the door wide open." I was still not myself completely. It was an out-of-body experience for me. As I got up from the floor, I closed the door and laid back on the middle of the living room floor.

I was back to reality when I woke up the next morning. I discovered that I was naked and there was vomit not too far from me. I was scrambling to find out what had happened to me because I felt that my body was different. I even went throughout the house to see if my friend was still there because he was the last person that I saw the previous night. I phoned my friend in a panic. I asked him, "Did anything happen last night with us? My body feels different and I don't remember anything." He said, "I walked you to your door and then left.

At that moment, so many emotions were going through my mind. I had never been in a place where I didn't recall anything or to the point where I would black out. The purpose for me going out last night was to take a load off my mind but I got more than I was expecting.

14
What's Familiar Can Kill You

That man raped me. It took me some time to say it. I was in complete denial about it for years. I literally had to go to therapy to acknowledge what happened to me that night.

I was not conscious of what was going on, the opportunity presented itself to do something that I didn't consent to, and I wasn't fully aware of what was taking place. Immediately, I became so angry to the point where I was yelling on the phone with my friend because I knew I wasn't crazy.

I began to shut down and became depressed because I didn't listen to the warning of the Holy Spirit. If I had listened, I would not have been in that situation. I felt so guilty. I stayed in friendships because of guilt. The support that I thought I would have in that moment was far stretched and led to manipulation. I have heard so many twisted words that were identified as "truth."

I had gotten to the point of quoting Bible scriptures in order to hide behind the insults that I would receive, saying that "God told me." I was to blame, in the eyes of other people, for what that man did to me and I didn't have the confidence to go beyond the fear of explaining my truth. But maybe the truth that I wanted to be explained wasn't necessarily the truth for anyone but me.

We can imagine ourselves in our hurts, mishaps, and even our disobedience by finding ways to distort where our true truth can lie. I had a traumatic experience at the hands of someone I thought would never do anything so cruel and bold. I did not adhere to the voice of God that placed me in danger. Even in that situation, He covered me with his grace.

15

Thorns Bring Scars Just for The View

The betrayal by my friend taught me to never allow my voice to become higher than God's voice. I didn't know what was going to happen to me but He did. It's important to adhere to God's warning before the warning is gone.

I remember vividly the conversations I would have that made me feel that "I had to be there for the other person who was hurting" rather than tending to my own needs for self-healing. You cannot heal yourself when you are bleeding. The more that I tended to a person who I thought was a safe place to express feelings, the more depressed I became. Insecurity increased and a sense of worth-lessness began to set in—not because of what had happened to me.

It was a combination of not listening and not leaving soon enough from unhealthy friendships in general—not just this one in particular. I recall dating a guy who didn't even claim me but was so emotionally distraught after all the things that he did to me. Facades play out well when no one knows your secrets.

A lot of times we don't truly see what we truly have and we don't appreciate all that we have until something happens. I remember the tears but that didn't move me. How many people can say that the people that they "hurt" or those who have "hurt" them stayed in a friendship with them because of guilt? I intentionally put the hurt in quotations because we oftentimes don't identify the hurt as well as we make excuses of that hurt. It definitely makes you look crazy on the outside when you continue to befriend that hurt. Know that what happened to you was not your fault.

You are strong and you should never let anyone make you feel less than that because of your truth! It's not okay. I was sexually assaulted as a freshman by an upperclassman in college. It scared me for a good minute about how I interacted with people but I still had to move forward.

I have so many life experiences that I have faced.

I don't know what may have happened in your life or whether it could be rape, molestation, substance abuse, fornication, depression, or emotional or physical abuse. Whatever trials you had made you who you are now because flowers can't be uprooted in soil if there isn't a firm foundation to stand on.

Part IV
Bloom

16

What They Thought Killed Me Produced More From Me

Nothing in this life is by accident or coincidence; all the way down to the very essence of who you truly are. The mistakes and the things which you have faced in life have embarked you on a whole new meaning.

The bloom is defined as something that is noticed, confident, and rare. Not too many people are aware of that special quality as it comes to the blooming stage when it produces flowers.

Your life is specifically designed for life circumstances, whether good or bad. Some difficult situations that you face in life are a setup so that the experience can be used by God to help others. Have you ever been at a place in your life where you needed guidance or help and, to your surprise, the person that you shared your problem with has been through a similar or a far worse situation?

Blooming means not being ashamed of your past or your present, your then, or your now. The bloom is the understanding of what life can be when you fully embrace it in confidence knowing, without a doubt, that the makeup of who you were created to be is a beautiful journey. I did not truly understand the blooming stage of life until I began working at a flower shop while writing this book.

The job came out of the blue because I had no desire to work with flowers or even learn about them. I actually got the job through a friend who told me God wanted me there and that I should apply for the position. I got the job and I learned so many things about how each individual flower or plant is processed, how they should be cared for, and whether they are indoor or outdoor flowers and plants.

I began to see the correlation between flowers

and how people live their lives. I've prepared flowers and plants for gifting and delivered them to those that were celebrating a new love, a loss of a family member, friends, funerals, new beginnings, new babies, and so much more. I enjoyed interacting with people the most in my job and didn't realize it was a part of my purpose. I soon developed an appreciation for the beauty in the journey and it taught me patience and confidence in my uniqueness and my efforts.

I have always loved pink roses but what I learned about the development of a rose when it's blooming, and even life after the bloom, was amazing. To watch the blooming stage of a rose is intriguing. How do you recognize that you are at the blooming stage of your life? You start to bloom when you get to a place of security and knowing that you are turning a new leaf in your life away from doubts, worry, and fear.

Flowers bloom in different seasons just like our lives. We just have to wait for our season. Waiting can be very challenging when you don't have anything to look forward to or you are going through so much that you can't see beyond where you are. You may ask, "How you can see the purpose beyond where you are?" First, recognize the stage that you are in — seed, thorns, or bloom.

The seed is the foundation of everything that you know. If the seed is not right or is not processing right, the manifestation of that seed might be slightly delayed if it is not receiving proper nutrients. Where you are planted matters. What's inside of you matters. It is up to you to decide how you will begin because seeds don't sprout overnight. Seeds are not made to look pretty on the outside because what's inside of them is far more valuable.

Roses bloom in the midst of thorns. In life, thorns are the core; the situations, hardships, and maturity as well as the development into all that you are purposed to be. Without thorns, there is no need to experience the bloom because the bloom is a result of the thorn. Just like you have a goal for the perfect body that is ideal to you and, although you may face some pain in getting that six pack or that booty sitting just right, in order to see results you have to go through vigorous workout pains.

Your thorns may be the result of the painful loss of a child, a heartbreak, a setback, a divorce, or a father or mother that wasn't there for you. Thorns are part of the beauty of life. Through the thorns, a bloom is produced. Anything that is not produced is not effective in contributing and building up the garden of life and impacting the lives of others.

In order to bloom and produce, you will need to deal with the DEAD roots in your life. Dead roots can hinder your growth process. Understand the seasons of your life and that the things you need deposited to survive will be the best for your growth.

17
It's A New Season

Winter, spring, summer, and fall are not just identified with earthly seasons but also the seasons of life. Life brings some cold and isolated days, warm and breezy days, hot and humid days, and the fall of life where you need self-evaluations.

Understanding seasons helps you to recognize that you have a hidden bloom inside of you that the world is waiting to see. Don't allow what you have been through, what people have said, or any struggles in your mind and heart to hinder you from what God has called and purposed for you to be. If you don't know where you are, or if you don't have an idea of where you are, its okay to feel that way. I really didn't know where I was until I began writing this book.

There is a reason for everything and a time and a season for clarity. I learned from my job at the flower shop that some people throw the rose away when it appears dead. They do not realize that there is still life at the core. The more you take off the dead rose petals, there is a block weeded in dirt and multiple seeds that can be replanted that can sprout a multitude of new flowers.

I need you to understand that no matter what life has thrown at you or what you feel that you are not capable of accomplishing, or what appears to be dying in your life, seeds are attached to it to help you bloom again. A hidden bloom is quite valuable and it's living inside of you.

Now, what's your story?

My Hidden Bloom

Never truly identified who I was.
From the start of my existence there was
not a trace,
I could see from what was.

Born with a vision of my own life's purpose,
But blind to the road I felt I wasn't even built for.
Empty promises, broken heart, denounces,
Led to my own self inflictions.

It hurts to battle with your own self-worth,
Lowered to tend to the hurt all around you,
Manifest itself to harm you.

Disguising itself as a nice, fine figure,
Bible in one hand but a heart of evil.
I admit it was my fleshly weakness,
That would over and over again leave me
restless.

I knew better.
Not even worth it, sis.
Not even worth it, bro.

How could this be?
Definitely lost and quite delusional,
I went into deep depression at moments,
Not knowing where I would be.

Then I would feel an immediate compression,
From the things that were planted inside of me,
That couldn't even grow . . . where it was
raining.
I felt like I was in a drought hiding from the
harvest,
I could see planted all around me.
Until one day, the rain fell on me.
All it took one drop in the cracks,
Where I was standing.

I started seeing my very beginnings,
My life experiences that led me straight to
growing.
It wasn't at all easy but I started to see a peek,
Through the cracks of my being and it started to
bloom.

I was no longer ashamed of what had happened
to me,
Because the bloom brought new life.
That new life was hidden and embraced,
Now the world can see my life bloom,
And unlock what's hidden inside of you wanting
to bloom.

P.O. Box 453
Powder Springs, Georgia 30127
www.entegritypublishing.com
info@entegritypublishing.com
770.727.6517

CPSIA information can be obtained
at www.ICGtesting.com
Printed in the USA
LVHW050047200820
663704LV00015B/454

9 781735 173993